a pocketful of

RHYME

Imagination for a new generation

2006 Poetry Competition for 7-11 year-olds

YoungWriters

Verses From
Southern Scotland
Edited by Annabel Cook

 Young**Writers**
First published in Great Britain in 2007 by:
Young Writers
Remus House
Coltsfoot Drive
Peterborough
PE2 9JX
Telephone: 01733 890066
Website: www.youngwriters.co.uk

SB ISBN 1 84602 748 9

Foreword

Young Writers was established in 1991 and has been passionately devoted to the promotion of reading and writing in children and young adults ever since. The quest continues today. Young Writers remains as committed to the nurturing of poetic and literary talent as ever.

This year's Young Writers competition has proven as vibrant and dynamic as ever and we are delighted to present a showcase of the best poetry from across the UK and in some cases overseas. Each poem has been selected from a wealth of *A Pocketful Of Rhyme* entries before ultimately being published in this, our fourteenth primary school poetry series.

Once again, we have been supremely impressed by the overall quality of the entries we have received. The imagination, energy and creativity which has gone into each young writer's entry made choosing the poems a challenging and often difficult but ultimately hugely rewarding task - the general high standard of the work submitted ensured this opportunity to bring their poetry to a larger appreciative audience.

We sincerely hope you are pleased with this final collection and that you will enjoy *A Pocketful Of Rhyme Verses From Southern Scotland* for many years to come.

Contents

Lauren Greer (10)   1

Colgrain Primary School, Helensburgh

Jamie Bernard (7)	1
Lauren Shepherd (9)	2
Megan Robertson (9)	2
Chloe Hassall (9)	3
Anders Gillies (7)	3
Erin Santry (8)	4
Reece Grant (7)	4
Ailie Grant (9)	5
Heather McNeill (8)	5
Penelope McKerron (9)	6
Ollie Smith (7)	6
Kirsty Bond (9)	7
Shania Beaty (7)	7
Jack O'Neill (8)	8
Jamie Matthews (7)	8
Kieran McGrath (9)	9
Emma Louden (8)	9
Lewis Grant (9)	10
Irum Arshad (7)	10
Savannah Thorley (8)	11
Courtney-Leigh Young (9)	11
Duncan Anderson (8)	12
Geraldine McCulloch (8)	12
Callum Diffey (9)	13
Libby Barmby (7)	13
Emma Robson (9)	14
Lucy Ashworth (8)	15
Megan Stewart (9)	16
Lauren Murray (8)	17
Alexander Currie (8)	18
Chloe Williams (7)	18
Lauren Wilton (9)	19
Scott Thompson (8)	20
Lucy Barmby (9)	21
Chloe Murray (9)	22

Harry Pearce (9)   23
Brandon Staff (8)   24

Gateside Primary School, Gateside
Aneesah Sheikh (9)   24
Rosie Hill (11)   25
George McConnell (11)   25
Graeme Dowie (10)   25
Shaun Craig (9)   26
Hazel Munro (11)   26
Damon Allan (10)   26
Emma Gillan (9)   27
Simon Webster (9)   27
Hannah Main (9)   27
Laura Clark (9)   28
Donald Graham (9)   28
Sam Barker (9)   28
Heather Gibson (9)   29
Charlotte Conway (8)   29
Lynsey Muir (9)   29
Matthew McConnell (9)   30
Emma Taylor (7)   30
Erin Hill (7)   30
Caitlin Johnston (9)   31
Jessica McConnell (7)   31
Mark Taylor (8)   31
Matthew Richmond (7)   32

Goldenhill Primary School, Clydebank
Jordan Kay (9)   32
Abbie Warrington (8)   32
Nicole Taylor (9)   33
Fiona Henry (8)   33
Ross Elder (9)   34
Heather McEwan (9)   34
Lisa Taylor (8)   34
Kern Donald (9)   35
Ruairidh Munn (9)   35
Lewis Jordan (8)   35
Meghan Bellshaw (8)   36
Liam Ramsay (7)   36

Rebecca McKernan (8)	36
Nicola McLelland (9)	37
Jennifer Hardy (8)	37
Rachel Busby (9)	37
Matthew Lester	38
Darren Johnston (6)	38
Rebecca Doherty	38
Jack Cranmer (7)	39
Chloe Carline (6)	39
Laura Allan	39

Hayocks Primary School, Stevenston

Connor Hatton (11)	40
Stacey Grayston (10)	40
Dale Boyd	40
Jack Holmes (11)	41
Jodi Gordon	41
Jordan Gordon	41
Nairn McDonald (11)	42
Demi Paterson (10)	42
David Cairns (10)	42
Nicola Shaw (11)	43
Caitlin Howie	43
Marc Gray (9)	43
Jamie-Lee Cresswell (11)	44
Kristine Frew (11)	44
Gemma Gibson (10)	44
Declan Kelso (11)	45
John MacDonald (11)	45

Lilliesleaf Primary School, Melrose

Kirsten Love (9)	45
Rachael Armstrong (10)	46
Naomi Love (10)	47
Joanna Forster (9)	47

Park Primary School, Stranraer

Rebecca McCulloch (9)	48
David Smith (8)	48
Ronan McMurtrie (8)	48
Leonna Jodie Thompson (8)	49

Alistair Henry (8)	49
Morgan Doyle (8)	50
Katie Bate (8)	50
Kristina Allison (8)	51
Leanne Branen (8)	51
Fraser Anderson (8)	51
Euan Caldwell (7)	52
Spencer Jardine (8)	52
Aiden Caughie (7)	53
Kelsey Scott (8)	53

St Joseph's Primary School, Stranraer

Rachel Drysdale (11)	54
Jade McCulloch (11)	54
Sean Clarke (10), Michael O'Connor & John McCusker (9)	55
Maila Soriani (11)	55
Fergus Lochhead (11)	56
Kirstin Smith (9) & Ashley MacKenzie (10)	56

St Kenneth's Primary School, East Kilbride

Scott Hernon (11)	56
Katie Fox (10)	57
Melissa Moir	57
Lucy Simpson (11)	58
Fiona Blackwood (11)	59
Shannan Rodger (11)	59
Ross Macfarlane (11)	60
Drew Malarkey (11)	60
Tony Kelly	61
Conor McDonald (10)	61
Niamh Conlon (11)	62
Maria O'Donnell (11)	62
Stephen Robson (11)	63
Stephanie Alexander	63
Ryan McKenna (11)	64
Zoë Kilcullen	64
Ryan Treanor (11)	65
Nico Cibelli (11)	65
Christopher Friel (11)	66
Kieran Stewart (10)	66
Kirsty Ferguson (11)	67

Shaun McBride (11)	67
Jordan Houston (10)	68
Colin McCluskey	68
Niamh Fleming (11)	69
Christopher Russell (11)	69

Sanquhar Primary School, Sanquhar

Carrie Connor (11)	70
Corey Lee Dewar	70
Jill Grierson (10)	71
Aidan Kerr (11)	71
Jamie Simpson (10)	72
David Tedcastle (11)	72
Jamie Shankly (11)	73
Murray McVey (11)	73
Christina McKenzie (11)	74
John Greenshields (11)	74
Bethany Gibson (11)	75
Mitchell Hodge (11)	75
Sarah Abbott (10)	76
Brad Candlish (10)	76
Graeme Jamieson (11)	77
Ashley Cook (11)	77
Judith Park (11)	78
Daniel Smith (11)	79
Ian King (10)	79
Elisha Esquierdo (11)	80

Stonehouse Primary School, Stonehouse

Katriona McLachlan (10)	80
Ruari McFie (9)	81
David Ferguson (10)	81
Fiona Baxter (10)	81
Heather-Louise Gillespie (9)	82
Rebecca Simpson (10)	82
Katy Allan (10)	82
Rachel Boyd (10)	83
Kerr Hamilton (10)	83
Hollie McGowan (10)	83
Ewan McTaggart (10)	84
Jade McCarrison (10)	84

Claire Sangster (10)	84
Simrut Uppal (10)	85
Gemma Clarkson (10)	85
Bethany Hatcher (10)	85
Craig Boyd (10)	86
Lynsey Quinn (10)	86
Jamie Biggar (10)	86
Ciaran Grant (10)	87
Michael Evans (10)	87

Victoria Primary School, Airdrie

Gary Ferrie (11)	87
Jordan Hill (11)	88
Clark Jarvie (10)	88
Glen Goldie (10)	88
James McGuinness (11)	89
Lee McGuire (11)	89
Karly Rae (11)	89
Chelsey Lafferty (11)	90
Raymond Kwok (11)	90
Alan Bruce (11)	91
Lucy Haviland (11)	91
Kumval Aziz (11)	91

Wallace Hall Primary School, Thornhill

Amy Hollingsworth (11)	92
Benjamin Goodrich (11)	92

Whitehirst Park Primary School, Kilwinning

Alex Jardine (10)	93
Laura Macnair (9)	93
Callum Boyle (10)	93
Connor Stevenson (10)	94
Graham Shield (9)	94
Sam Hogg (10)	95
Stuart Faulkner (10)	95
Megan Rainey (9)	96
Craig Bruce (10)	96
Emma Hedley (10)	97
Andrew Whyte (10)	97
Jacqueline Reid (10)	98

Adam Hodge (9)	98
Kiara Henderson (10)	99
Gaynor Beaton (10)	99
Gemma Speirs (10)	100
Chloe McNulty (10)	100
Lucy Dyson (9)	101
Rohail Hamid (10)	101
Fiona McAllister (10)	102
Blair Wilson (10)	102
Jamie Kane (10)	103
Ross Pilling (10)	103

Woodlands Primary School, Irvine

Amanda Johnston (11)	104
Lauren McGill (11)	104
Louise Miller (11)	105
Andrew Gow (11)	105
Katie Bremner (10)	106
Anthony James Chalmers (11)	106
Kimberley Dean (11)	107
Rebecca Greenwood (11)	107
Kyle McDade (11)	107

The Poems

The Scary, Stormy Traveller's Night

(Inspired by 'The Listeners' by Walter de la Mare)

'Let me in,' shrieked the traveller,
Kicking on the icy smashed-in gate.
And then he stopped for a moment,
Wondering if he should wait.
As insects crept and crawled at his feet,
He cried, 'Let me in before it's too late.'

He heard footsteps running towards him
He banged with all his might.
He heard a faint howl far away
He didn't want to get in a fight.
The full moon shone over the dark clouds,
Sooner or later there would be no light.

A scream deafened his ears,
He had no one to tell.
The village was silent
Except from a loud, faint yell.
He knew that he was being haunted,
It was worse than living in Hell.

Lauren Greer (10)

The Battle

I see people dead and I see flaming arrows in the sky
I see swords stuck in the ground
I hear people screaming
I hear swords clicking
I hear people shouting for help
I feel scared, I feel fear, I feel sad
I wish that I could go home
I wish that it was over
I wish that I could run away.

Jamie Bernard (7)
Colgrain Primary School, Helensburgh

My Horse Bert

As fat as an elephant
As greedy as a cow
That's my Bert.

As cheeky as a monkey
And high as a gate
That's my Bert.

As funny as a clown
And fast as lightning
That's my Bert.

Orange, like a pumpkin
And as silly as my teacher
That's my Bert.

As cute as a hamster
And as brown as a nut
That's my Bert.

Lauren Shepherd (9)
Colgrain Primary School, Helensburgh

The Sea On A Stormy Day

The sea on a stormy day,
Bashes like a drum,
Crashes like a cymbal,
It never stops rolling.

The sea on a stormy day,
Crashes on the stones,
Then sucks back up,
It never stops rolling.

The sea on a stormy day,
I like to watch it,
Crash on the rocks,
It never stops rolling.

Megan Robertson (9)
Colgrain Primary School, Helensburgh

My Brother Murray

As loud as a hammer
As tall as a table
That's my brother.

AS cheeky as a monkey
And funnier than a clown
That's my brother.

Likes to eat chips
Likes to eat curry
That's my brother.

Jumps on the trampoline
Then lies on the ground
That's my brother.

He likes to play football
And he likes to play trains
That's my brother.

Sleeps on the sofa
Then snores like a train
That's my brother.

Chloe Hassall (9)
Colgrain Primary School, Helensburgh

The Battle

I see knights battling
I see swords banging
I see arrows shooting
And I see archers in bushes
I hear knights shouting
I hear swords and arrows banging
I feel ill, I feel very sad and I feel angry
I wish it was over.

Anders Gillies (7)
Colgrain Primary School, Helensburgh

My Dog Murphy

As cute as a mouse
Smaller than a doll's house
My dog Murphy.

He likes to eat treats
But not chocolate sweets
My dog Murphy.

He sleeps all day long
To keep nice and strong
My dog Murphy.

He lays on the floor
Then jumps at the door
My dog Murphy.

The best friend I've got
We love him non-stop
My dog Murphy.

Erin Santry (8)
Colgrain Primary School, Helensburgh

The Battle

I see fighting knights,
Lots of swords, silver armour,
I hear metal crash, people shouting for help
And people screaming,
I feel sick with fear,
Really scared and very angry,
I wish this could stop.

Reece Grant (7)
Colgrain Primary School, Helensburgh

That's My Mum

Kind as an angel
Tall as a blackboard
That's my mum.

Eats all her spinach
And washes the dishes
That's my mum.

Gives me a hug
And a kiss goodnight
That's my mum.

She tidies my room
But not with a broom
That's my mum.

I hug her a lot
And kiss her non-stop
That's my mum.

Ailie Grant (9)
Colgrain Primary School, Helensburgh

The Battle

I see lots of lots of dead people on the ground
Lots of helmets lying on the ground
And lots of people running away
I hear people calling for help
And lots and lots and lots of banging
Lots of people are screaming
I feel sad
I wish my friends wouldn't get hurt.

Heather McNeill (8)
Colgrain Primary School, Helensburgh

My Niece Megan

Cute as a puppy
Still uses her nappy
That's my niece.

She's nearly walking
And halfway to talking
That's my niece.

She eats lots of fruit
And her toys go toot
That's my niece.

As much fun as a swing
And sometimes sings
That's my niece.

I kiss her a lot
And love her non-stop
That's my niece.

Penelope McKerron (9)
Colgrain Primary School, Helensburgh

The Battle

I see flaming arrows in the sky
And dead people on the ground
And the knights fighting for good
I hear people shouting, swords click, clash, and fire crackling
I feel scared and sad but angry too
I wish this could stop.

Ollie Smith (7)
Colgrain Primary School, Helensburgh

My Friend Lucy

She is so friendly
But not so trendy
My friend Lucy.

Louder than a mouse
When she's at my house
My friend Lucy.

She is very nice
She doesn't like spice
My friend Lucy.

She likes having fun
When there is some sun
My friend Lucy.

She will always pat
Her two gorgeous cats
My friend Lucy.

Kirsty Bond (9)
Colgrain Primary School, Helensburgh

The Battle

I see lots of knights fighting,
Flaming arrows and shining armour,
I hear swords crashing,
Screaming and knights shouting,
I feel really scared, sick and terrified,
I wish this could stop.

Shania Beaty (7)
Colgrain Primary School, Helensburgh

My Brother

As tall as a car
As fast as a cheetah
That's my brother.

Eats like a horse
Swims like a fish
That's my brother.

Fun as an Xbox
As cool as a shark
That's my brother.

As loud as a foghorn
As bony as a snake
That's my brother.

Loves to play football
Likes to play in the park
That's my brother.

Jack O'Neill (8)
Colgrain Primary School, Helensburgh

The Battle

I see lots of dead people
And some fighting knights and lots of swords
I hear some swords crashing
And some metal banging and people screaming
I feel sick with fear and really scared and very angry
I wish that this had never happened.

Jamie Matthews (7)
Colgrain Primary School, Helensburgh

My Dog

As cute as a baby
As white as the snow
That's my dog.

Funny as a clown
Fluffy as a rabbit
That's my dog.

Eats lots of her treats
Loves them like her meat
That's my dog.

Jumps on my dad's back
Scratches him on the face
That's my dog.

Loves her bones like me
On her bed she lies
That's my dog.

Kieran McGrath (9)
Colgrain Primary School, Helensburgh

The Battle

I see fighting and lots of shields and flaming arrows
I hear lots of noise and people shouting, people moaning
I feel sad, miserable and angry
I wish this had never happened.

Emma Louden (8)
Colgrain Primary School, Helensburgh

My Brother Mark

As kind as a teacher
As big as a house
That's my brother.

Likes to watch TV
Likes to eat fish
That's my brother.

Runs as fast as a car
Washes the dishes
That's my brother.

Sleeps in the bed
Snores like a lion
That's my brother.

Fun to play with
Funnier than my dad
That's my brother.

Lewis Grant (9)
Colgrain Primary School, Helensburgh

The Battle

I see dead people and lots of shields and lots of swords
I hear metal crashing and people screaming and people crying
I feel sad, scared and upset
I wish my friend was safe.

Irum Arshad (7)
Colgrain Primary School, Helensburgh

My Cousin

She has thick curly hair
Likes yummy chocolate
That's my cousin.

She plays tennis
And she misses the ball
That's my cousin.

She loves all the boys
She kisses them lots
That's my cousin.

She loves shopping
She shops till she drops
That's my cousin.

She doesn't like football
She can't kick a ball
That's my cousin.

Savannah Thorley (8)
Colgrain Primary School, Helensburgh

The Battle

I see people are dead and my friends are dead
I hear shouting and crying
I feel I want to run away
I wish it would never happen again.

Courtney-Leigh Young (9)
Colgrain Primary School, Helensburgh

My Cat Chiang

As brown as chocolate
As mad as a monkey
That's my Chiang.

As quick as lightning
As strong as a lion
That's my Chiang.

Likes to eat snacks
And also eggs
That's my Chiang.

As clean as soap
And smelly like flowers
That's my Chiang.

He plays with glee
As loveable as me
That's my Chiang.

Duncan Anderson (8)
Colgrain Primary School, Helensburgh

The Battle

I see dead people
Knights fighting, they have silver armour
I hear people shouting very loud and lots of people screaming
I feel very frightened and sad
I wish that there were no battles.

Geraldine McCulloch (8)
Colgrain Primary School, Helensburgh

My Cat Molly

She's as soft as wool
She jumps at the fridge
That's my Molly.

She likes TV
She jumps on me
That's my Molly.

She loves fish
But not on a dish
That's my Molly.

She plays with wool
Doesn't go to school
That's my Molly.

She rolls on the floor
Till she hits the door
That's my Molly.

Callum Diffey (9)
Colgrain Primary School, Helensburgh

The Battle

I see dead people, flames in the sky
I hear lots of noise when they battle
I feel very sad because some of my friends are dead
I wish this could stop and this had never happened.

Libby Barmby (7)
Colgrain Primary School, Helensburgh

My Cat Sam

Fat as a rat
And lies on the mat
That's my Sam.

He likes treats
And he likes sweets
That's my Sam.

He chases the girl cats
But not the rats
That's my Sam.

He lies on my bed
And purrs at my leg
That's my Sam.

When he's bad
He gets very sad
That's my Sam.

He is sweet as can be
When he sits on my knee
That's my Sam.

Emma Robson (9)
Colgrain Primary School, Helensburgh

My Cousin Samantha

She's born on Hallowe'en
And she's as bossy as a queen
My cousin Sam.

She's really quite lean
But hardly ever mean
My cousin Sam.

She's got a cute smile
And she can run a mile
My cousin Sam.

She's very good at badminton
And also cheerleading
My cousin Sam.

She will eat up all her food
And scoff up all her pud
My cousin Sam.

I love her a lot
I'm full of love to the top
My cousin Sam.

Lucy Ashworth (8)
Colgrain Primary School, Helensburgh

My Guinea Pig Taty

As loud as a whistle
As small as my foot
That's my Taty.

Likes to eat apple
And carrots and leaves
That's my Taty.

Runs like the wind
And as nice as an angel
That's my Taty.

As white as a sheep
With caramel dots
That's my Taty.

More fun than a clown
She has no frown
That's my Taty.

The best friend I've got
I adore her a lot
That's my Taty.

Megan Stewart (9)
Colgrain Primary School, Helensburgh

My Fish

As big as a pencil
As thin as one too
That's my fish.

As fast as lightning
As quiet as a mouse
That's my fish.

As good as gold eating his food
As brown as a nut
That's my fish.

He doesn't like getting out of the tank
When it's getting cleaned
That's my fish.

He's a nice fish
And moves like a snake
That's my fish.

He has lots of cool toys
And he likes to play
That's my fish.

Lauren Murray (8)
Colgrain Primary School, Helensburgh

My Brother

Loud as a car
Big as a tree
That's my brother.

Funny as a clown
Faster than me
That's my brother.

Sleeps on the sofa
Then snores like a train
That's my brother.

Washes his car
Then mows the grass
That's my brother.

Likes to eat chips
And curry ice cream
That's my brother.

Alexander Currie (8)
Colgrain Primary School, Helensburgh

The Battle

I see shining silver armour and lots of flaming arrows, knights, fighting
I hear swords clashing and people shouting, 'Stop this,'
                              and people yelling
I feel really scared and very sad and very, very angry
I wish my friends were safe.

Chloe Williams (7)
Colgrain Primary School, Helensburgh

My Snake Bourny

He's as black as a panther
And as smooth as silk
That's my snake.

As mad as a monkey
As funny as a clown
That's my snake.

As cheeky as a monkey
As nice as a rose
That's my snake.

Sleeps like a log
He's hard to wake up
That's my snake.

Even if he's bad
We still love him
That's my snake.

Lauren Wilton (9)
Colgrain Primary School, Helensburgh

My Friend Matthew

He's always very fun
When we play PS2
My friend Matthew.

As funny as a clown
We're always up, not down
My friend Matthew.

We're never very sad
After all the fun we've had
My friend Matthew.

We like to eat sweets
And chocolate treats
My friend Matthew.

Runs as fast as me
As we chase the bees
My friend Matthew.

Scott Thompson (8)
Colgrain Primary School, Helensburgh

My Mum

She loves us so much
And we love her too
That's my mum.

Her favourite food's apples
And chips and rice
That's my mum.

She's as big as a shop
She cleans with a mop
That's my mum.

Her make-up is everywhere
Clothes are on the chair
That's my mum.

Her bag is full
There's stuff everywhere
That's my mum.

Lucy Barmby (9)
Colgrain Primary School, Helensburgh

My Sister

She's fat as a cat
And sits on the mat
That's my sister.

She's as small as a bee
And sits on my knee
That's my sister.

She eats lots of sweets
And loses her treats
That's my sister.

She's very cheeky
And jumps like a monkey
That's my sister.

She's as sweet as sweets
When she sits on my knee
That's my sister.

Chloe Murray (9)
Colgrain Primary School, Helensburgh

My Brother Tom

As good as an angel
And is really smart too
That's my brother.

Likes to play golf
And is as good as the Tiger
That's my brother.

Likes to eat chips
Likes to eat curry
That's my brother.

Likes to play pool
And is really cool
That's my brother.

He's got really good jokes
And never lets me down
That's my brother.

Harry Pearce (9)
Colgrain Primary School, Helensburgh

My Pets

My cat is sleeping
So is my dog
That's my pets.

My dog sleeps a lot
So does my cat
That's my pets.

My dog likes his food
My cat likes his food
That's my pets.

They like to play chase
They curl up together
That's my pets.

They like to growl
And my cat goes purr
That's my pets.

Brandon Staff (8)
Colgrain Primary School, Helensburgh

Kangaroo

Kangaroo, hop around like mad,
    Kangaroo, you're being bad,
        Kangaroo, stop embarrassing me,
            Kangaroo, won't you come to tea?
        Kangaroo, there's something in your pouch,
    Kangaroo, ouch! Ouch! Ouch!
Kangaroo, you are getting too mucky,
    Kangaroo, why aren't you lucky?
        Kangaroo, you're making me laugh,
            Kangaroo, you do need a bath,
        Kangaroo, are you having fun?
    Kangaroo, isn't that a big sun?
Kangaroo, would you be my friend?
    Kangaroo, I'll call you Ben.

Aneesah Sheikh (9)
Gateside Primary School, Gateside

Pony Club

P op on the pony and away we go
O ver the jump and a clear round it is
N othing to worry about, just sit back and relax
Y ork show . . . first goes to us

C ool cuddly ponies
L ong lush manes
U nbeatable gallop
B onding together makes a good team.

Rosie Hill (11)
Gateside Primary School, Gateside

My Dog

My dog is a puppy, Jack Russell-cross
What it's crossed with is anyone's guess.
All I know is he loves the guests
He eats his food then goes to bed.
He could sleep through a thunderstorm
He had a puppet, he ripped out the stuffing
But through it all I love him
Because he's my dog.

George McConnell (11)
Gateside Primary School, Gateside

Budgies

B udgies live in a cage,
U sually budgies swing and sing,
D rinking water from their bowl,
G rowing big and eating lots of seed,
I n the cage, day and night,
E njoying having company,
S inging, talking all day long.

Graeme Dowie (10)
Gateside Primary School, Gateside

Dogs

Dogs have furry coats
And have fun
They are friends.
Dogs eat too much
And run too fast
They are very playful
My dog's name is Cali
Cali chews his ball
We throw the ball for him
He loses his ball.

Shaun Craig (9)
Gateside Primary School, Gateside

Dancing Is Great

D ancing is great
A cro, tap and jazz
N ever get bored
C lap your hands with the music
I mmediately tap your feet
N eed all the shoes to do the dancing
G reat fun and a good way to keep fit.

Hazel Munro (11)
Gateside Primary School, Gateside

The Zebra

The zebra will jump if you give it a fright
But when you scare it, it'll be back
The zebra's the one that will be right
And you're the one that's stepped on the tack
But be aware of its awesome might
And never scare them when they're in a pack.

Damon Allan (10)
Gateside Primary School, Gateside

School Time

S pelling can be hard
C ool classes
H ard work we have to do
O rganised work laid out for us
O ther stuff we like to do
L isten carefully, but work hard

T ick-tock says the clock
I think it's now playtime
M rs McKay is my teacher
E verything has been done.

Emma Gillan (9)
Gateside Primary School, Gateside

Running

R enfrewshire is where I run
U nusual people can run too
N othing is better than running
N ever stop exercise
I like to run in my garden
N ight is a time I don't run
G oing for a run is fun.

Simon Webster (9)
Gateside Primary School, Gateside

Horses

H orses gracefully galloping in the field
O rders the people give them, they do not come
R iders sit on the saddle, the horses go and run
S addles and saddles. They don't come they just want to run about
E very horse will be good if you are nice to them.

Hannah Main (9)
Gateside Primary School, Gateside

Friends

F riends forgive each other,
R olling and playing in the grass.
I n winter friends always play
E ven in the snow, rain and sleet
N o one will be left out so join in the fun
D oing things inside and out
S ummer days are the best in the pool, having water fights.

Laura Clark (9)
Gateside Primary School, Gateside

Collies

C ollies are black and white
O n my farm I have some collies
L ots of collies need
L ots of food, some of the time I feed the dogs
I like collie dogs
E xcellent collies are the best
S ome are brown and white.

Donald Graham (9)
Gateside Primary School, Gateside

Spaniel

S oft and fluffy as a cloud,
P uppy spaniels are the cutest in the world.
A lfie is deaf to everything apart from the call of his stomach
N aughty puppy gets what he deserves
I gnorant puppy steals from the table
E ats to his heart's content
L azy puppy lies on the couch.

Sam Barker (9)
Gateside Primary School, Gateside

After School

After school,
The chalk sings a song
And the rulers stretch,
After lying in a box all day long.

The scissors and glue,
Dance to the song by chalk,
And all the books,
Go for a walk!

It's an amazing thing,
After school is.
So when the bell rings . . .
Remember this!

Heather Gibson (9)
Gateside Primary School, Gateside

Little Bunny

B eautiful brown bunny with a white fluffy tail
U nder the straw she hides
N ever bites anyone
N ibbles her food in the morning and at night
Y ou'd want a bunny like mine.

Charlotte Conway (8)
Gateside Primary School, Gateside

Horse

H aving a roll in the field
O ut in the fresh air, in the grass
R acing horses going as fast as they can over the bushy jumps
S tallions, mares and geldings, lots of different kinds
E at lots of hay, carrots and grass.

Lynsey Muir (9)
Gateside Primary School, Gateside

History

V ikings loved adventure and saw the chance in a new land
I nvading countries for new land and more food
K eeping bad spirits away which would help win the battle
I nvincible till they went to Largs for more land
N ever managed to take Largs! So . . . they scattered
G olden eagle's head to scare away bad spirits and the enemy
S candinavia is the name of the three countries they came from.

Matthew McConnell (9)
Gateside Primary School, Gateside

Rabbits

R abbits are cuddly, lovely and cute
A rabbit needs lots of company
B unnies just need a little food
B unnies can do backflips, my bunny can do them
I like my rabbits and they have a big run
T hey need lots of exercise every day
S o I love my Bubbles very much.

Emma Taylor (7)
Gateside Primary School, Gateside

Horse

H andsome, tall, standing up high
O ats are what they like to eat
R unning around in the fields like mad
S ense of hearing and sniffing so good
E normous, he stands like a giraffe.

Erin Hill (7)
Gateside Primary School, Gateside

Giraffe

G iant creatures, yellow with black spots
I n the countryside having fun
R unning from place to place so tired out
A big, big animal that is very tall
F antastic, big, big animals
F rolicking in the countryside
E nough space for a big giraffe.

Caitlin Johnston (9)
Gateside Primary School, Gateside

Eagle

E xciting, extraordinary wings flying high in the sky
A mazing creatures these birds that I want to know
G lide, great, great predators and hunt a lot
L ong legs, long gliders, live long, not lonely
E xciting, flying and gliding, extraordinary length of wings.

Jessica McConnell (7)
Gateside Primary School, Gateside

Snowy Owls

S ensational, snowy birds soar through the sky
N octurnal birds the lot of them
O n top of the trunk they look after their sons
W e only really see them in snowy places
Y ellow some owls are

O bedient birds they are too
W arm, soft creatures fly through the night
L ovely white owls, time to go to sleep.

Mark Taylor (8)
Gateside Primary School, Gateside

Eagle

E xciting, extraordinary wings flying high in the sky
A mazing creatures these birds I want to know
G lide, great, great predators and hunt a lot
L ong legs, long gliders, live long, not lonely
E xciting, flying and gliding with extraordinary length of wings.

Matthew Richmond (7)
Gateside Primary School, Gateside

Hallowe'en

H allowe'en is the best
A t Hallowe'en you dress up
L ights all over my garden
L anterns all over my garden too
O n Hallowe'en my party is scary
W e go trick or treating
E verywhere we go on this night
E veryone gives us treats
N o more time, I've got to go!

Jordan Kay (9)
Goldenhill Primary School, Clydebank

Flowers

Flowers live in gardens
Flowers grow from seeds
Flowers, of course we sleep
There are so many like me
I am a weed, so pretty and sweet
Sorry, this is the end of me.

Abbie Warrington (8)
Goldenhill Primary School, Clydebank

Family Poem

Family is my parents
Family is my aunt
Family is my uncle
Family is my cousin

I like my family because I stay at my aunt's
At the weekend and we bake fairy cakes.

Family is my parents
Family is my aunt
Family is my uncle
Family is my cousin

My family is my uncle and I like my uncle
Because I stay at weekends and watch TV.

My family is my parents and I love them.

Family is my parents
Family is my aunt
Family is my uncle
Family is my cousin.

Nicole Taylor (9)
Goldenhill Primary School, Clydebank

Christmas

Christmas isn't about the presents or the food
It is about what happened over 2,000 years ago
On 25th December, in Bethlehem
But why didn't they have turkey or wine?
Because nobody knew He'd be born
So the next time you have a Christmas party
Don't just care about the presents
Think about the true meaning of Christmas.

Fiona Henry (8)
Goldenhill Primary School, Clydebank

The Sun

The sun is shiny like glitter
The sun is hot like a fire flicker
The sun is bright and warm
It will always be the same
The sun heats you up when you're cold
The sun watches you when you're old
The sun will come to an end
And it will disappear and that's the end.

Ross Elder (9)
Goldenhill Primary School, Clydebank

Who Am I?

Who am I?
I flutter by
Floating on air
Without a care
I land on flowers
But to me like tall towers
Who am I?
A butterfly.

Heather McEwan (9)
Goldenhill Primary School, Clydebank

The Chick

In an egg was a little chick
It started to crack
Out came a chick
The mother was happy
It was quite cute
The dad came along, he got a fright
It was like love at first sight.

Lisa Taylor (8)
Goldenhill Primary School, Clydebank

A Witch's Recipe

You will need:
2 spiders
A monster
3 slugs
2 mugs
1 snail
Some ale
A pinch of dust
Some rust.

1 Put two spiders and a monster in a cauldron
2 Add a snail and some ale
3 Put in dust, rust, a bottle of worms and some thumbs
4 Heat for an hour then put in some slugs
5 Put into some mugs
6 Eat.

Kern Donald (9)
Goldenhill Primary School, Clydebank

My Friends

My friends are always there to help me
They always care the most when I am hurt
They're always there to help me
Sometimes I get in a mood and lose my good friends
But we always make it back up.

Ruairidh Munn (9)
Goldenhill Primary School, Clydebank

Motorbikes

Motorbikes fast and slow, everywhere I go
Wheelies up and down the hills, everywhere I go
The engine buzzing mega loud, everywhere I go
I enjoy being on my bike, everywhere I go.

Lewis Jordan (8)
Goldenhill Primary School, Clydebank

Teacher

Teacher, teacher
Always talking
Teacher, teacher
Never stopping

Sit up straight
Stop talking
Open your books
And start copying

It's home time now
Get your shoes
Get your bag
And go!

Meghan Bellshaw (8)
Goldenhill Primary School, Clydebank

Love

Love sounds like the birds singing
Love tastes like bees
Love smells like perfume
Love looks like a heart
Love is the colour red
Love reminds me of birds.

Liam Ramsay (7)
Goldenhill Primary School, Clydebank

Christmas

Christmas is cold
Christmas is fun
Christmas has toys and fun, fun, fun
Christmas is cool
Christmas rules
Christmas is fun for kids to rule.

Rebecca McKernan (8)
Goldenhill Primary School, Clydebank

Chocolate

C ream filling
H ot melting chocolate
O utstanding cream
C adbury's is the best
O rdinary flavour
L ove it
A lways yummy
T astes delicious
E specially nice.

Nicola McLelland (9)
Goldenhill Primary School, Clydebank

Fireworks

Fireworks are so beautiful
Fireworks are so colourful
Fireworks are green, red, blue and yellow
Fireworks can be as yellow as a star
Fireworks are so bright they can shine at night
Fireworks, fireworks, fireworks
How beautiful can they be!

Jennifer Hardy (8)
Goldenhill Primary School, Clydebank

Fireworks

Fireworks are flickering through the sky
Fireworks are bursting with beautiful colour in the air so high
Fireworks can be noisy and loud but it's fun to see
the fireworks explode
Bang! Boom! Boom! The fireworks go off, it's amazing
Fireworks can be yellow, blue, white and green
The prettiest colours I've ever seen
Fireworks, fireworks will always be the best thing for me!

Rachel Busby (9)
Goldenhill Primary School, Clydebank

Untitled

Love sounds like kisses
Love tastes like steak bakes
Love smells like beans
Love looks like a rugby pitch
Love is the colour red
Love reminds me of my gran's cat.

Matthew Lester
Goldenhill Primary School, Clydebank

Love

Love sounds like my mum's voice
Love tastes like bananas
Love smells like sausages
Love looks like a heart
Love is the colour red
Love reminds me of my nana.

Darren Johnston (6)
Goldenhill Primary School, Clydebank

Love

Love sounds like a bird
Love tastes like Smarties
Love smells like a rose
Love looks like a butterfly
Love is the colour of red
Love reminds me of my fish.

Rebecca Doherty
Goldenhill Primary School, Clydebank

Love

Love sounds like a monkey
Love tastes like cherries
Love smells like a hot dog
Love looks like a heart
Love is the colour red
Love reminds me of a hamster.

Jack Cranmer (7)
Goldenhill Primary School, Clydebank

Love

Love sounds like romance
Love tastes like hot chocolate
Love smells like a rose open
Love looks like a rose petal
Love reminds me of my family
Love's colour is red.

Chloe Carline (6)
Goldenhill Primary School, Clydebank

Love

Love sounds like loud noises
Love tastes like chocolate
Love smells like hot chocolate
Love looks like a rabbit
Love is the colour blue
Love reminds me of my mum.

Laura Allan
Goldenhill Primary School, Clydebank

Blue

Ribbons twirling round
Pencils that you draw with
The sky on a beautiful summer's morning
A tropical sea
Paint to decorate a house
Birds singing in a rainforest
Blu-tack sticking to the wall.

Connor Hatton (11)
Hayocks Primary School, Stevenston

What Is Red?

It reminds me of juicy tomatoes.
Parrots with very long, sharp beaks.
Fireworks exploding.
Wobbly jelly.
It is the colour I go when I feel embarrassed.
Strawberries - the best fruit in the whole wide world.

Stacey Grayston (10)
Hayocks Primary School, Stevenston

What Is Green?

Long grass on the field
Balloons flying in the air
A clown's hair
My football team
Grapes growing on a vine
A lizard climbing on a bunch of leaves
A punk's hair everywhere.

Dale Boyd
Hayocks Primary School, Stevenston

What Is Blue?

Bright summer sky.
Sea in the sunlight.
Feathers of blue jays.
Real Madrid and Rangers all dressed up.
Balloons in the air.
Special vinyls on a Mitsubishi.
Folders taking up space.
Books in a library.
Trays on a shelf.
Water bottles holding juice.

Jack Holmes (11)
Hayocks Primary School, Stevenston

Blue

Balloons flying high
Bright and bold
Folders on a shelf in a straight line
Light sky in the summer season
Water of the oceans, seas and lakes
Raindrops when the weather is not good
The calm sea in the summer.

Jodi Gordon
Hayocks Primary School, Stevenston

What Is Blue?

Bright skies in the middle of summer
Chelsea and Manchester City
Rain falling into big puddles
Ferrari zooming by
Cheese and onion crisp packets
Berries, juicy and bright.

Jordan Gordon
Hayocks Primary School, Stevenston

Indigo

Beautiful summer mornings.
Juicy sweet grapes.
Wine so fine.
Hummingbirds like rich jewels.
One of a rainbow's graceful colours.
Amethyst - so gorgeous.
Winter clothes.
Summer fruit - juicy and sweet.
Calm and relaxed is how it makes me feel
When embarrassment runs through my veins.
My cuddly teddy.
And that's *indigo!*

Nairn McDonald (11)
Hayocks Primary School, Stevenston

What Is Blue?

Rangers football strips.
My favourite colour of car.
Balloons flying high.
Book covers.
Water - seas, rivers, oceans.
Rain falling from the sky.
A parrot flying in the rainforest.

Demi Paterson (10)
Hayocks Primary School, Stevenston

Untitled

There once was a small boy called Matt
Who owned an amazing, smart rat.
That night it got out.
It ran all about.
Unlucky - right into a cat!

David Cairns (10)
Hayocks Primary School, Stevenston

What Is Red?

Gorgeous sunset.
Balloons flying high.
Folders on shelves.
Juicy, small tomatoes.
Cupid's arrows.
Gushing bright blood when you cut yourself.
Fast, bright cars zooming by.
Ready salted crisp packets.
Shiny, red, juicy apples on a tree.

Nicola Shaw (11)
Hayocks Primary School, Stevenston

What Is Green?

Long grass in summer
Leaves mean starting a new life
Jealousy
The colour you feel when you come off a roller coaster
Emeralds glittering in a ring
The colour of juicy grapes
Rainforests
The colour of a witch's face at Hallowe'en.

Caitlin Howie
Hayocks Primary School, Stevenston

Untitled

There once was a rabbit called Marc
Who always went out in the dark.
It was such a pain
When it started to rain.
But he danced round the park for a lark.

Marc Gray (9)
Hayocks Primary School, Stevenston

Green

Green.
The colour of the swishing trees.
Made to sway by an awful breeze.
Long, long grass.
Juicy grapes.
In shops a display of winter capes.
Green is the nicest colour
I've ever seen.
Beans.
Exploding fireworks.
You - when you have just been sick -
Yuck!

Jamie-Lee Cresswell (11)
Hayocks Primary School, Stevenston

What Is Red?

My favourite colour.
Tomatoes, juicy and bright.
A Valentine heart.
A wobbly jelly.
A healthy heart.
One of the colours of the rainbow.
A colour of a parrot in the rainforest.

Kristine Frew (11)
Hayocks Primary School, Stevenston

Untitled

There once was a cat called Fred
Who slept on a loaf of brown bread.
He once met a frog
Who slept on a dog.
They now own a big double bed.

Gemma Gibson (10)
Hayocks Primary School, Stevenston

Untitled

There once was a girl called Annie.
Whose dad had a job as a jannie.
She went to the beach
Where she ate a peach.
Then she went home to her granny.

Declan Kelso (11)
Hayocks Primary School, Stevenston

Untitled

There once was a cute cat called Maisy
Who was terribly tired and terribly lazy
She went to the mall
And bought a huge ball
Now Maisy is crazy.

John MacDonald (11)
Hayocks Primary School, Stevenston

Fairy Tales

Fairies going up and down streets,
The king talking to everyone he meets.

Giants going weak,
A bird with a big long beak.

Princesses all dressed up,
A prince with a little pup.

Fairy tales always being made,
Fairy tales always being saved.

Kirsten Love (9)
Lilliesleaf Primary School, Melrose

The Four Seasons

Just as winter disappears the bleating of lambs comes to my ears,
Farmers' crops are being sown
And April showers are being blown,
All the kids are out to play, so thank you for this fine spring day.

Now that spring is out the picture and summer is here at last,
All the lambs are fully grown,
Their bleats are in the past,
Ice cream vans around the park
And kids playing on the swings,
The sun is at its highest peak watching over all these things.

The summer sunshine disappears,
Autumn is coming fast,
The flower heads are closing and the leaves are getting past
And when you look up in the sky the birds are flying south
And I see a blue tit with a berry in its mouth.

Frosty rings upon your window,
Cold toes in your bed,
Could it be a sign of winter?
Are Santa's reindeer fed?

Santa wears his big red coat,
Sitting in his sleigh,
The year has nearly ended
Now it's Christmas Day.

Now I have told you about the seasons,
In my little rhyme,
There is always one around the corner
Through the passing of time
So to finish my little poem do a favour for me
And remember this little rhyme in your memory.

Rachael Armstrong (10)
Lilliesleaf Primary School, Melrose

Once Upon A Time

Once upon a time is a poem about fairy tales
It is set in an enchanted wood
There's sometimes some winds and sometimes some gales
And I think it's pretty good.

Once upon a time there stood a yellow wee fairy
Swishing her long white wand
She was standing at the front of a chocolate dairy
Waiting beside the pond.

Once upon a time there lived a chubby green elf
Who always let his kids around loose
Who only cared for his house and himself
Then one day turned into a goose.

Once upon a time there lived a pink princess
With a dazzling shiny crown
Who always made an untidy mess
And lived in a faraway town.

Once upon a time was a poem about fairy tales
It was set in an enchanted wood
There's sometimes some winds and sometimes some gales
And I think it's pretty good.

Naomi Love (10)
Lilliesleaf Primary School, Melrose

The Grey Mare's Tail

Swooshing water falling down, trying not to make a sound
Climb up if you dare! Try not to trip over a hare
Lovely water flowing fast, lots of people walking past.

Splishing, sploshing, everywhere, Daddy shouts and says, 'Take care!'
When all the water has flown away, we jump in the car and drive away.

Joanna Forster (9)
Lilliesleaf Primary School, Melrose

My Funky Box
(Based on 'Magic Box' by Kit Wright)

I will put in my box . . .
The smell of a beautiful flower
A taste of a morning dew
A stormy sea as the waves crash against the rocks
A sound of the birds tweeting.

I will put in my box . . .
The feeling of a happy child
A dream of a grown-up having a sleep
The roar of a lion.

Rebecca McCulloch (9)
Park Primary School, Stranraer

My Magic Box
(Based on 'Magic Box' by Kit Wright)

I will put in my box . . .
Eggs, boys playing, pigs singing
Dragons breathing fire, knights in shining armour
A sandstorm from the beach, a witch on a white horse
The sound of the ocean from the deep blue sea
A stamp from a giant, a noise from a T-rex.

David Smith (8)
Park Primary School, Stranraer

My Bongo Box
(Based on 'Magic Box' by Kit Wright)

I will put in my box . . .
A tiger with no teeth, a bird that can't fly
And a fish that doesn't swim.

I will put in my box . . .
The sound of the ocean breeze
The sound of a thousand beating drums.

Ronan McMurtrie (8)
Park Primary School, Stranraer

My Mega Box

(Based on 'Magic Box' by Kit Wright)

I will put in my box . . .
A bendy spoon
And a huge bouncy balloon
The feeling of the dragon's fire hitting your head.

I will put in my box . . .
The smell of the ocean sea.

I will put in my box . . .
The shining sun that can't shine
Dreams that can't come true
Food that you cannot chew.

I will put in my box . . .
A lion that cannot roar.

I will put in my box . . .
The smell of when you're first born.

Leonna Jodie Thompson (8)
Park Primary School, Stranraer

The Box Of Flames

(Based on 'Magic Box' by Kit Wright)

I will put in my box . . .
A golden dragon egg
Flesh of a human's body
The horn of a unicorn.

I will put in my box . . .
Lightning that will not strike
The smell of Granny's feet
The sadness of a house on fire.

My box is made of the flames of a Hungarian dragon
The hinges are made of bulls' horns.

Alistair Henry (8)
Park Primary School, Stranraer

My Smelly Box

(Based on 'Magic Box' by Kit Wright)

I will put in my box . . .
A smelly carpet
A smelly couch
Smelly chips.

I will put in my box . . .
Some blood and the feeling of a sad girl
And the sound of the sea.

I will put in my box . . .
The thunder of forked lightning
The dream of a monkey.

I will put in my box . . .
The smell of lovely roses
An animal with no legs
The taste of delicious roast beef.

I will put in my box . . .
The taste of burnt toast.

Morgan Doyle (8)
Park Primary School, Stranraer

My Mad Box

(Based on 'Magic Box' by Kit Wright)

I will put in my box . . .
A balloon that will not burst
And a zoo with a code.

I will put in my box . . .
Dreams that come true
And the smell of a gingerbread man coming to life.

Katie Bate (8)
Park Primary School, Stranraer

My School Box

(Based on 'Magic Box' by Kit Wright)

I will put in my box . . .
A flying pencil
A flying book
A flying teacher.

I will put in my box . . .
Rain
Cold
A pen which is invisible.

Kristina Allison (8)
Park Primary School, Stranraer

My Wacky Box

(Based on 'Magic Box' by Kit Wright)

I will put in my box . . .
A flying toenail
A very scary dream
A scary freaky sound
A very creaky sound of thunder
A magic flying tiger.

Leanne Branen (8)
Park Primary School, Stranraer

The Amazing Box

(Based on 'Magic Box' by Kit Wright)

I will put in my box . . .
The ghostly, lonesome feeling on Hallowe'en day
A glowing star from the sky above
The snowy mountains from the land afar
A small curly banana
And the roar of a sabre-toothed tiger.

Fraser Anderson (8)
Park Primary School, Stranraer

My Weird Box

(Based on 'Magic Box' by Kit Wright)

I will put in my box . . .
A magic trick
A talking mouse that lives on my shoulder
A magic metal fist
A screech from a T-rex
The strike of a lightning bolt
All power orbs from planet Ranger
The smell of petrol
A petal from a blast flower
The cake that cannot go away.

Euan Caldwell (7)
Park Primary School, Stranraer

My Clown Box

(Based on 'Magic Box' by Kit Wright)

I will put in my box . . .
A sand monster that can fly
A thunder tornado hitting buildings down
The smell of the sun
The smell of Gran's feet
A chicken that breathes fire
A man dressed up as food
The smell of petrol
A scream of a tyrannosaurus rex
A sun that is black.

Spencer Jardine (8)
Park Primary School, Stranraer

My Crazy Box

(Based on 'Magic Box' by Kit Wright)

I will put in my box . . .
Lightning that can't strike
Rain made of blood
A rotten toe cut off
A monkey that can't swing
A bee that can't fly
Cheese you can't cut
Cheese that you can't go near or you will die
A sound that is so loud that you can't hear
Rain that goes backwards
Deep snow that you can't fall through
A radiator that goes cold
Dogs that speak funny
And that can't make you laugh.

Aiden Caughie (7)
Park Primary School, Stranraer

My Invisible Box

(Based on 'Magic Box' by Kit Wright)

I will put in my box . . .
A lovely shiny sun
A shiny black and white zebra.

I will put in my box . . .
A smell of yellow flowers.

I will put in my box . . .
A feeling of a smooth animal's leg.

I will put in my box . . .
Dreams that aren't true.

Kelsey Scott (8)
Park Primary School, Stranraer

Autumn

The leaves change from green to brown
Then they flutter to the ground
Hallowe'en comes, we all dress up
And knock on our friends' doors
Shouting
Trick or treat!
We all get candy, a lolly or two
Our toffee-coated apples as hard as stone
Then, five days later, we all look up into the dark sky
And suddenly . . .
Boom! Crackle!
Beautiful colours fill the sky
Pink, white, purple, red and blue
Autumn is nearly over
Can't wait to start again next year.

Rachel Drysdale (11)
St Joseph's Primary School, Stranraer

Autumn

In autumn the leaves fall down
In a whirl of red, gold and brown
Outside in the garden
In the crisp white frost
I feel warm in my jumper
As I pick up seeds
Apples as ripe as the ones you get in the shop
Leaves covering the garden like a blanket
In my bed I am as cold as a freezer
I can't sleep, the wind is as loud as a tumble dryer
When I wake up I run outside
To find the dew is sparkling in the sun.

Jade McCulloch (11)
St Joseph's Primary School, Stranraer

Weather

The rain started to fall
Everyone in their houses
Take in the new ball
Get out of the playhouses.

The wind blew like a leaf blower
The trees boogied about
We helped to take in the mower
We fished for some trout.

The street was filled with mist
The leaves were fiery red
The trees all had a twist
But all the leaves were dead.

The colder days had a misty morning
The breeze started to cool my head
Sitting under big tall trees
Goodnight all, I'm off to bed.

Sean Clarke (10), Michael O'Connor & John McCusker (9)
St Joseph's Primary School, Stranraer

Autumn

Leaves falling gently down
Conkers lying on the grass, shiny as a new penny
All the trees are bare
Walking through the colourful leaves
Crunchy, crunch, crunch
Rain starts, wind picks up
Leaves fly, trees sway
Getting dark, shorter days
Dew like glitter on the grass.

Maila Soriani (11)
St Joseph's Primary School, Stranraer

Autumn Poem

Wind whistling through the air
Trees sway from side to side
Leaves blowing about the garden
Waves crashing upon the shore
Days start to get shorter, cooler
Conkers covering the flower bed
Birds start to fly south
Leaves all coloured red.

Fergus Lochhead (11)
St Joseph's Primary School, Stranraer

Weather

Leaves rushing in the breeze
The autumn mist is making me sneeze
The rain is drumming, my head is giving me a pain
The water flows down the drain
The hailstones are banging off the tin roof
The nights are getting cooler in the autumn.

Kirstin Smith (9) & Ashley MacKenzie (10)
St Joseph's Primary School, Stranraer

Roller Coaster

I'm waiting in the queue, excitement setting in
A few minutes now and then the fun begins
Slow to start, we make our way to the top
My heart beats faster as we head for the drop
Hands shaking, palms sweaty, my mind goes blank
The cart turns into a thundering tank
The wind crashes upon my face
As I feel I've survived a drop from space.

Scott Hernon (11)
St Kenneth's Primary School, East Kilbride

From My Window I Can See

From my classroom window I can see . . .
A huge bare tree as tall as can be
A tall, dirty lamp post standing up proud and straight
Singing, colourful birds just back from a bathe in the sea.

From my bedroom window I can see . . .
The local swimming pool, that's where I want to be
Little people passing by, they look as small as ants
A lovely little park hiding amongst the trees.

From my car window I can see . . .
All the other cars passing past me
Tall lamp posts starting to turn on
Car lights staring, as scary as can be.

We are so lucky that we can see
So you should be as happy as me!

Katie Fox (10)
St Kenneth's Primary School, East Kilbride

Autumn

The air is cold, the leaves are red and gold
As they flutter to the ground
Creating a crispy, crunching sound

The birds and animals flee to their homes
While the fir trees let go of their precious
Fir cones

Walking along down the leaf-covered path
Kicking them up and having a laugh
Strolling through the park what can I see?

I can see the colours of the leaves
And the dogs barking at the birds
In the trees.

Melissa Moir
St Kenneth's Primary School, East Kilbride

The View From My Window

From my bedroom window I can see
The huge oak tree
Looking back at me
I love to look out in autumn
As the leaves fall to the bottom.

From my car window I can't see a thing
It's frozen up with ice
It really is freezing
But if I roll it down
I can see the snow and ice
It's so nice.

From my classroom window I can see
The budding flowers and birds that sing
All these new things tell me it's spring
With longer light and warmer days
And all the children out to play.

From my hotel window I can see
The sandy beach and the deep blue sea
Summer's here
It's time to cheer and put on your fancy swimming gear.

All these things I can see
As the seasons change around me!

Lucy Simpson (11)
St Kenneth's Primary School, East Kilbride

Autumn Poem

As I walked through the forest
The trees looked like chocolate men
The ground was like a river of leaves
The hills looked like an avalanche of grass!

The clouds were like candyfloss
There were apples in the tree like jelly beans
It felt like Jack Frost
Had cast a spell on the forest.

The flowers were like lollipops
Rain from the trees fell like lemon drops
The bushes were like rolls of seaweed
Autumn is the best season!

Fiona Blackwood (11)
St Kenneth's Primary School, East Kilbride

From My Window I Can See . . .

From my window I can see . . .
The beautiful sea with fish swimming to and fro
And sand moulding into the shape of children's footprints.

From my window I can see . . .
People from the market buying and selling things
Children coming and going to and from school.

From my holiday window I can see . . .
Babies and mothers playing in the pool together
Adults sitting down watching children play
All of this is happening around me.

Shannan Rodger (11)
St Kenneth's Primary School, East Kilbride

When I Look Out Of My Window

When I look out of my window I can see
A huge and gnarled old oak tree
Going up like a wave
A creature we must save
This is what I can see all around me.

When I look out of my window I can see
The sky in which all things are free
From the great eagle
To a small seagull
This is what I can see all around me.

When I look out of my window I can see
A cloud like a jellyfish in the sea
White and lovely
Or dark and angry
This is what I can see all around me.

Ross Macfarlane (11)
St Kenneth's Primary School, East Kilbride

My Window

From my window I can see
Singing birds on the old oak tree
Cars zooming past as fast as ever
And fish leaping in and out of the river.

From my bedroom window I can see
The big yellow sun smiling at me
And clouds like candyfloss as far as I can see
Lamp posts so tall and bright
Oh, looking out my window, what a wonderful sight.

So if you see the things that I see
You can be happy just like me!

Drew Malarkey (11)
St Kenneth's Primary School, East Kilbride

Autumn

As the autumn days go by the trees go bare.
The days get shorter and the nights get longer.
The leaves fall like confetti
And a kaleidoscope of colour.

The leaves rustling every step I take
And when I wake I make a mistake
And go back to sleep
Because it is darker in the morning.

The colour of the leaves are
Ruby, orange and brown.
Autumn is the lead up to Hallowe'en.

Tony Kelly
St Kenneth's Primary School, East Kilbride

A View From My Window

From my classroom window I can see:
The black and dirty birds eating the bread
The tall and bushy trees swaying in the winter wind
And the long and straight lamp posts looking at me.

From my bedroom window I can see:
The bright and colourful fireworks sparkling in the sky
The big and demanding house looking at me
And the green grass sitting beautifully in the garden.

From my car window I can see:
Nothing but the cold and icy window
Rotting with the manky flies and the cold seats making me shiver.

Conor McDonald (10)
St Kenneth's Primary School, East Kilbride

Autumn Is Here

Autumn is here in all of its beauty
Bronze, ruby and amber leaves plucked off the trees by the wind
And pirouetting round and round.

Conkers are out of their prickly cases
Children collect and test them
Apples and other fruits are ready to be picked and eaten.

Hallowe'en is to follow, ghosts, ghouls and witches
Are ready to fly and children go trick and treating
The night is eerie and the wind howls.

The night is long and the moon is high
Everywhere is cold and dark
Only the sun, moon and bulbs ignite the sky.

Niamh Conlon (11)
St Kenneth's Primary School, East Kilbride

Autumn Poem

A tornado of colourful leaves,
Days getting colder,
Nights getting longer.

A kaleidoscope of colours,
Leaves crunching,
Clocks going back.

A patchwork quilt of fallen leaves,
Amber, brown and ruby,
Animals hibernating in their holes.

A crunching sound when you step on leaves
The run up to Hallowe'en,
The wind howling like wolves in the night.

Maria O'Donnell (11)
St Kenneth's Primary School, East Kilbride

Autumn

All the trees are swaying in the cold autumn breeze,
Around me I see piles of brown and gold leaves,
The days are getting darker and cooler
And the breeze is nipping my neck and my shoulder.

When I see the morning dew,
It tells me the day has come anew
And the animals are all snug in their holes,
I have some warm soup with rolls.

Everyone is excited for spooky Hallowe'en
And the days are getting shorter it might seem,
All the leaves are raked into a bunch
And the children walk through them with a *crunch, crunch, crunch.*

In my house I feel all warm,
But outside there's a blizzardous storm,
Hallowe'en is very near,
But even better, autumn is here.

Stephen Robson (11)
St Kenneth's Primary School, East Kilbride

Untitled

Creatures are carefully planning their hibernation
Cold as it creeps closer to winter
Comfortable people in their houses with blazing fires
Children jumping in leaves
Autumn is golden.

Days getting shorter, nights getting longer
Darkness is cold and eerie
Dreaming about winter, snow and Christmas
Dreary nights occur in autumn
Autumn is red.

In my eyes that's how I see autumn!

Stephanie Alexander
St Kenneth's Primary School, East Kilbride

Autumn Poem

Leaves fall, conkers come
Hallowe'en is great fun
Weather changes, brollies fly
Grey clouds in the sky
Leaves pile up, we kick them high
In America we eat pumpkin pie!

The nights are longer and the moon is high
The stars are shining in the sky
Everywhere is dark and spooky
The wind gets stronger
As the moon comes out longer.

The leaves start to change colour
Ruby, orange, brown and golden
Just like looking through a kaleidoscope
Autumn sounds, *crunch, crunch, crunch*
Autumn's here
Autumn's here.

Ryan McKenna (11)
St Kenneth's Primary School, East Kilbride

Autumn

Leaves falling from the trees,
Bronze, amber, ruby, gold,
It's like a big swimming pool of leaves,
The nights are getting colder, days getting darker.

The witches and devils will soon be seen,
Summer and spring have already been,
Everyone loves our Hallowe'en.

Conkers falling from the trees,
Conkers is our favourite game
And conkers is the real name,
Autumn is the best, and Santa comes next!

Zoë Kilcullen
St Kenneth's Primary School, East Kilbride

Autumn Poem

Autumn is here and everyone is out playing
Walking home leaves are crunching beneath me
Leaves falling off trees like confetti
Making a patchwork quilt of amber, bronze and ruby.

Trees starting to get naked by the minute
Days getting colder, nights getting darker
And I'm coming in earlier
Kids diving in and out of a hill of golden leaves
Collecting conkers to play the game in winter
May as well get them while we can.

Leaves caught inside a whirlpool of wind
Rustling on the ground
All the leaves making a kaleidoscope of colour.

It's the run up to Hallowe'en.

Ryan Treanor (11)
St Kenneth's Primary School, East Kilbride

Autumn

Autumn, autumn, what a season, leaves flying everywhere
Underground rabbits getting ready for winter
The leaves are turning golden-brown
Undergrowth mushy underfoot
Nuts and chestnuts now on sale

Trees getting bare by the second
The days get colder and the nights get darker
A strong wind is howling like a wolf
A whirlwind of leaves spinning round and round like a spinning top.

Crusty leaves crunching like stepping on crisps
Amber, ruby and bronze leaves caught in a swirling wind
Autumn is here and summer is gone.

Nico Cibelli (11)
St Kenneth's Primary School, East Kilbride

Autumn Poem

Say goodbye to summer,
Cos autumn's on its way,
Birds are going away,
And we don't want to play.

The leaves patchwork the ground,
Rusty red, amber and bronze,
Lie dead on the path,
The swirling winds blow them around and round.

Kids look forward to Hallowe'en,
Someone will probably go and scream,
I got some candy off a dirty old hag,
She chucked it into my swag bag.

Animals are in their snug little holes,
Badgers retreat for hibernation,
Seldom chance you will see a mole,
Whilst mist covers our whole nation.

Christopher Friel (11)
St Kenneth's Primary School, East Kilbride

Autumn

Children rustling in the leaves.
Whirlpools of litter and leaves.
All the days are getting colder.
Colours of brown, ruby and amber.

Clearing away for winter nights.
Wind howling in the night.
Getting darker in the morning and night.

Tidying up the messy garden.
Coming up to Hallowe'en.
Birds and animals migrating for the winter.
Autumn is here!

Kieran Stewart (10)
St Kenneth's Primary School, East Kilbride

Autumn

As the leaves fall off the trees
Autumn begins
Full of surprises
A different surprise for each new day
The swirling wind
The rustling of the trees

A whirlpool of leaves filling the autumn air
A kaleidoscope of colour
Ruby, amber, bronze, golden
Animals snug in their holes
The birds flying to new countries
For more heat

Oh, how I can't wait till Hallowe'en
All the costumes
Children trick or treating
Lots and lots of chocolate and sweets
Wondering what I am dressing up as
Oh, how I love autumn!

Kirsty Ferguson (11)
St Kenneth's Primary School, East Kilbride

Autumn Poem

The lead up to Hallowe'en was colder and darker,
The rustling and crunching sound ruled the street,
The amber, bronze and golden leaves were the street's colour.

Howling wind and a tornado of leaves
At the end of a long wide street,
Hallowe'en getting closer.

Naked trees surrounded with a tornado of leaves
In the strong whistling wind.
But the most amazing sight,
The confetti of colourful leaves.

Shaun McBride (11)
St Kenneth's Primary School, East Kilbride

Autumn

Autumn mornings and autumn nights
From September to October
Rain no shine

All the puddles on the ground
And people splashing like they're in a water park
Splish, splash, the birds are in the bath

After a bath it's time to fly south
Then time for a spooky party
Last year I got 2 bags of fruit and 3 bags of sweets.

Jordan Houston (10)
St Kenneth's Primary School, East Kilbride

Autumn Poem

Leaves along the floor like a patchwork quilt of colour,
Days are colder as it comes near winter,
The leaves crunch under my feet as I go to school.

Animals run back to their snug little holes to hibernate.
Bronze, ruby and amber leaves fall like confetti from the trees,
Children get costumes for the run up to Hallowe'en.

Dogs bark at the birds perched in the tree branches,
Leaves everywhere like a kaleidoscope of colour,
Raking them up from the garden.

Colin McCluskey
St Kenneth's Primary School, East Kilbride

Autumn Poem

The nights start to get darker
As the days start to get colder
Everyone is starting to wear hats, scarves and gloves.

The boys and girls are jumping in the leaves
The trees suddenly get bare
But nobody really cares.

Some people are starting their holidays
Autumn is ending
But winter is beginning.

Niamh Fleming (11)
St Kenneth's Primary School, East Kilbride

Autumn

The days get shorter,
The days get colder,
Piles of crunchy leaves,
Orange, gold and red,

Twisting and turning through the air,
How silently they tumble down,
Children jumping in and out
Of the piles of leaves.

Autumn is coming to an end,
But winter is coming, *whoopee!*
Autumn is fun!

Christopher Russell (11)
St Kenneth's Primary School, East Kilbride

Ma Pal Jill

Ma pal's name is Jill
She has got broon hair
Glesses n bloo een
She has dodgy spelling.

Ma pal Jill joost lives
Twa doors up fae me
'N' she likes tae huv
A gid laff.

Ma pal Jill is a lot
Bigger thin me and
I think she is as
Big as a tree.

Ma pal Jill hus
A cool car 'n' she
Always eats an
Irn-Bru bar.

Carrie Connor (11)
Sanquhar Primary School, Sanquhar

Ma Pal Daniel

Ma wee pal Daniel
He sees the geed in everythin'
He likes these wee monster guys
Who shoot fireballs at each other.

Daniel's hobbies are hockey, two-wheeling and archaeology
He always goes diggin' fer bones.

Ma pal Daniel
He has sky-high lugs
He's tall, wae black hair
It sticks up aw uver the bit.

Me an' Daniel goin' swimming every week
Daniel's no alod down the deep end
'Cause he cannie swim a length.

Corey Lee Dewar
Sanquhar Primary School, Sanquhar

Bout Wee Beth

Beth the biggest
Mooth in the town
But she like playing the clown
And her ears are like two big jugs
Her front teeth are like big mugs.

Her hoos is like a rat hole
And her dad looks like a mole
Their car is so rusty it goes bang
And her sister talks slang.

Beth thinks she gid at jokes
But she thinks I smell of socks
Beth is wee as a flea
But I am big as a bee

But ma hoos is like a rat hole.

Jill Grierson (10)
Sanquhar Primary School, Sanquhar

Mark is Ma Pal

Mark is ma pal
Ave ken Mark fur a lang time
I cannae remember when I met him
We bathe was wee
We sterted skool the same day.

Mark ayways play wae me
I think he's awfaey kind and gid
He sties very neer tae me
I'm doon below him
I can hear aw his bangs.

We play at skool and at ma hoose
We luv oor PlayStation 2
We gan on the trampoline
We play at any game.

That's why Mark is ma pal.

Aidan Kerr (11)
Sanquhar Primary School, Sanquhar

Ma Pal Jamie

He makes me laugh does Jamie
He is quite silly sometimes though
Whenever he hurts his pinky toe
And when he's on his trampoline
He's always like a mean machine.

His eyes and hair are baith broon
When we are looking doon the toon
His personality is quite good
Whenever he's running roon the hood.

We were in Jamie's room
When someone came in the room
It was his mum
Wantin' him to feed the guinea pig.

That's ma pal Jamie.

Jamie Simpson (10)
Sanquhar Primary School, Sanquhar

Ma Pal Poem

I huv a wee pal called Jamie
He's got hair a bit like me
An although his rather tall ma wee brother likes him tae
He's aye gan on aboot how spotty he is
But he feels like a pal to me.

He always thinks he's funny
But that's no' how it is at all
In fact he's rather silly at times
But he cun be clever tae.

We've made up oor own wee radio station
We've got a website for it tae
We sometimes gan oot boardin'
Al playing on the PlayStation an' all.

I suppose he is kinda a funny wee guy
Well that's ma pal.

David Tedcastle (11)
Sanquhar Primary School, Sanquhar

Ma Wee Pal Jamie

Ma wee pal cried Jamie
His hair is broon
And is een are tae
That's just like me
We make a super pare.

He came roond tae ma bit wance
We wereny takin' care
He fell and hit the table
And landed on the flare.

Jamie is a happy chappie
He always keeps us happy
He's usually really silly
But that's what maks him Jamie.

Jamie Shankly (11)
Sanquhar Primary School, Sanquhar

Wee Jimmy

Dae yae ken ma pal Graeme?
But we jeest caw him Jimmy
Se when he gets something aboot fitball
He takes it well too far.

He's a wee shrimp
In aw he likes fir his lunch is buttered rolls
He's a Rangers fan bit takes it too far
In when we play fitball it the primary
He's nay confidence in hisself.

See sometimes he kin be a right pain
And sometimes talks back
Actually quite aloat of the time.

And when we're no' playin' fitball
He drives yae up the wall
Saying dae yae want tae play fitball?
No, mibbe after.

Murray McVey (11)
Sanquhar Primary School, Sanquhar

Ma Pal Elisha

Ma wee pal Elisha isnae very big
Her feet are tottie an' her hair is short
Noo her hair is a mix ae colours
Wae blonde 'n' a broony colour, bit it's nice.

She might run fast but she runs slow as oot
Elisha cun be funny
Bit maest ae the time she acts stupid
Din annoy her ar she'll blow
Half the time she looks daft
'Cause her lug rings an specks dinnae match.

Wae go loads ae bits the gither
Ice skatin' wis yin ae the bits wae went bit she kept fallin'
Et the park I can't get tae come awa fae it
Wae like gone tae parties an' discos the gither tae.

An this is ma wee pal Elisha Esquierdo.

Christina McKenzie (11)
Sanquhar Primary School, Sanquhar

Ma Pal Jack

Ma pal Jack
He cun rin like the wind

His hair is bland like cream
He's gut lit blue eyes
But he is gonnae have tae put meat on
He's skinny

He plays fly half
Because he can flee
He rins at such a pace

I huv wun six gowden medals wi' him
Wi' him in the team we cannae lose
But he always scares mare points than me
But he is still ma pal.

John Greenshields (11)
Sanquhar Primary School, Sanquhar

Ma Freen Elisha

Ma freen Elisha
She's eva sae funny
She makes me laugh every day
Her funniness lasts twenty-four/seven, sae does her grin.

Well she's only gan an hus tanned skin
An broon an black specks
Her een are broon tae
She also hus broony blonde shilder length hair
I'm startin' tae think her favourite colour's brown.

Whit we dae when we play
Well we ither gan skateboardin'
Or we gan tae the park
She usually gans roon ma hoose instead.

I've never bin roon her house, no' even yin tim
She mit be hidin' somethin' awa fae me
I just wantin' tae get in their fae myself
I ken I'll get in there yin day.

Thit's ma freen Elisha.

Bethany Gibson (11)
Sanquhar Primary School, Sanquhar

Ma Pal Graeme

Ma pal Graeme is wee and roon
His face is nae a pretty sight
He is always happy and cheers me up when I'm doon
We always play fitba.

When we play fitba it is always very fun
Even though he always wins
When we play tig I always catch him
Graeme is nae a fast runner.

Graeme is nae stupid
But still he's no' the brightest chap
So that's ma pal Graeme.

Mitchell Hodge (11)
Sanquhar Primary School, Sanquhar

Ma Pal Jemma

Ma big pal Jemma
Is only 11 years auld
She always calls me silly
And never stops talkin at all.

Her hair is broon
And she always has it up
She always weers too big a jeans
And never weers shorts
But never matchin socks.

Wa always go tae a park
She always says, 'Iv got spin syndrome.'
When wi go on the roonaboot
It's the same a the time.

But every marnin at 8
Ring goes ma phone it's Jemma
Meet me at the skool
And that's ma pal Jemma.

Sarah Abbott (10)
Sanquhar Primary School, Sanquhar

Ma Pal Scott

Ma pal Scott keeps on losin' the plot
He's goat a gid right fit
He's sometimes a pain and weighs
Six 'n' a half stane.

We play fur the same team
He's gid et golf
He's goat a big brother cod Liam
That's ma pal Scott.

Brad Candlish (10)
Sanquhar Primary School, Sanquhar

Ma Pal

I've kent ma pal since he wis a bairn
He's aff his blond heid
He needs a richt guid feed
He is awfy lanky
Oaften manky.

He's no the brichtest o' folk
He hates the schuil
He hus a dug caad Bruce
For ye're ain guid, dinnae lit him loose.

He's no' very braw
He kens he-haw
He's no' bad at fitball
That's Murray McVey for ye.

Graeme Jamieson (11)
Sanquhar Primary School, Sanquhar

Ma Best Pal

Dae ye want tae ken ma best pal?
Ma best pal's ma mum
She's the best pal ye can ever get
Ma wan an' only mum.

Ma maw's got short broon hair
Wae a smile fae ear tae ear
Her legs are lanky long
A bit like mine
But nae body still canny beat ma mum.

She's really funny an' daft
But her laugh's like a snorting pig
Still nae body's mum's like mine
Ma smiling, kind, best pal.

Ashley Cook (11)
Sanquhar Primary School, Sanquhar

Ma Pal Bobbie

Ma freen Bobbie
In ma class
Never see 'er frownin
Blonde hair, 11 year ol'
'N' she grins fae ear tae ear.

Every Friday we muck aboot it each ithers hoose
'N' all tell ye this
The things we daw
Hidin', riding, biking
Evin golfin!

Yin time on a bright summer's day
Wae went tae the pictures tae see Harry Potter
But the best bit wis when   .
We went tae the toilet
Bit the head tae the screen hid chinged
'Cause it hid nearly finished
So we panicked bit in the end we funit.

But then when we got back in
Wae got cote up
'N' tripped ower 'n' ower
'N' let oot a shreek
Bit who's kidden, wae did get a row
And goen hame that night wis
Funny telling the story again and again.

Judith Park (11)
Sanquhar Primary School, Sanquhar

Jamie

Ma pal Jamie has an awfy big heid
His eyes are broon an' his hair is tae
The feet are far tae big, I think he's size 11
But he says he's only a 5.

Jamie thinks he's funny but he's no' really
Silly is far mair like the word
Right enough he's awfy guid at poetry
And writing is his thing.

We havenae spent a lot o' time tegether
Ye see a live in the country
But at schule we a'ways play
Tig an' sometimes fitba'.

Daniel Smith (11)
Sanquhar Primary School, Sanquhar

Jim-Bob

Jim-Bob ma freen Jim-Bob
He's nearly bald
He's kindae wee
Wae short black hair
He geeze me brooses that ie sairer than saire.

We had a rubber fight in the class
Wae rubbers missin' ma head
I wis sure a wis naan bread

We've had some fun
We've laught 'n' laught
But ae always ken
Jim's dafter than daft.

Ian King (10)
Sanquhar Primary School, Sanquhar

Ma Pal Christina

Di ye ken ma pal Christina?
She hus broon hair, it's quite long
Green een she hus got
She is really tall, size five fit.

She is real crazy, smart tae
She's real funny a'ways
Disnae like being told wit tae dae
She is a real fast runner

There is load o hings we've dun together
Like ice skating and discos
Yin time at ice skating she fell

There's loads ae hing she likes
White chocolate she luvs 100%
An astra belts she likes

Noo ye ken ma pal Christina.

Elisha Esquierdo (11)
Sanquhar Primary School, Sanquhar

Darkness

I woke up in complete and utter darkness
It followed me around all day
All that black, it drove me mad,
It would drive you crazy too
I ran as fast as I could all the way home from school
With the faint taste of blood in my mouth
Everything looked like a lonely planet with just an alien for company
I felt like I was trapped inside a freezing block of ice
I was haunted by my own nightmare, I'd had the night before
Then I woke up . . . I was still in darkness
Argh!

Katriona McLachlan (10)
Stonehouse Primary School, Stonehouse

Anger

Anger is red like a new car
It sounds like a lion roaring for its dinner
It tastes like a chilli pepper going down your throat
It looks like a bush on fire in the forest
It feels like your hair is burning
And it reminds me of my teacher yelling at me.

Ruari McFie (9)
Stonehouse Primary School, Stonehouse

Happiness

Happiness is yellow like the sun
Happiness sounds like a beautiful song
Happiness tastes like your favourite food
Happiness looks like your favourite football team winning the cup
Happiness feels like you're on a cruise
Happiness reminds me of playing football.

David Ferguson (10)
Stonehouse Primary School, Stonehouse

Sadness Is Like . . .

Sadness is blue
It sounds like someone playing a slow piece of music with a violin
It tastes like icy cold blue berries
It looks like a cloudy grey sky
It just feels like a soaring emptiness in your stomach
It reminds me of a lonely blue balloon floating in the night sky.

Fiona Baxter (10)
Stonehouse Primary School, Stonehouse

Anger Is Red

Anger is red
It sounds like thunder crashing in the night sky
Anger tastes like salt getting poured into my mouth
It looks like a grizzly bear attacking a wild boar
Anger feels like a fire roaring in an empty room
And it reminds me of a battle.

Heather-Louise Gillespie (9)
Stonehouse Primary School, Stonehouse

Happiness

Happiness is yellow and blue
Happiness sounds like birds singing in the trees
Happiness tastes like chocolate éclairs melting in your mouth
Happiness looks like a scorching sunny day
Happiness feels like a lot of fun
Happiness reminds me of my new wee baby cousin.

Rebecca Simpson (10)
Stonehouse Primary School, Stonehouse

Anger Is Like . . .

Anger is red
Anger sounds like a motorbike running on the track
Anger tastes like a hot and spicy vindaloo chilli
Anger looks like a burning onion
Anger reminds me of the war.

Katy Allan (10)
Stonehouse Primary School, Stonehouse

Happiness

Happiness is yellow like the sun
Happiness sounds like the laughter of children
Happiness tastes like a never-ending chocolate cake
Happiness looks like a bunch of red roses
Happiness feels like the warmth of the sun
Happiness reminds me of love.

Rachel Boyd (10)
Stonehouse Primary School, Stonehouse

Anger

Anger is black
It sounds like loud thunder in the sky
It tastes like hot chilli soup in your mouth
It even looks like red blood
And it feels like a burning headache in your head
And it reminds me of my teacher.

Kerr Hamilton (10)
Stonehouse Primary School, Stonehouse

Happiness

Happiness is baby-pink
It sounds like the birds chirping, chirping, chirping in the trees
It tastes like sugar and spice and all things nice
It always looks like the sun shining in the sky
And the flowers in the green, green grass, colourful, colourful
It feels like a comfortable pillow in the night
It usually reminds me of a pretty rainbow shining beautifully in the sky.

Hollie McGowan (10)
Stonehouse Primary School, Stonehouse

Darkness

Darkness is the colour of eerie jet-black
Darkness sounds like the silence of a deserted place
Darkness tastes like freezing, icy cold air
Darkness looks like a gloomy night sky
Darkness feels scary like being in a haunted house
Darkness reminds me of a sound of a badger burrowing in soggy
ground.

Ewan McTaggart (10)
Stonehouse Primary School, Stonehouse

Anger

Anger is the colour of burning red
It sounds like a brand new motorbike racing along the road
It tastes like a spicy hot pepper in my mouth
It looks like fire blazing in the night sky
And it feels uncontrollable like a wild horse
It reminds me of a devil.

Jade McCarrison (10)
Stonehouse Primary School, Stonehouse

Love At Its Best

Love is baby-pink
Love sounds like the car not starting in the morning
Love tastes like ice cream and lollies on a hot day
Love feels like cuddling my sister all day long
Love reminds me of shopping and eating out at my
favourite restaurant.

Claire Sangster (10)
Stonehouse Primary School, Stonehouse

Fun

When I am having fun I am playing football
Or eating my favourite food which is marshmallows
                              with melted chocolate
And it looks like the sun shining down
And it sounds like party music
And the best thing is it reminds me of fun.

Simrut Uppal (10)
Stonehouse Primary School, Stonehouse

Anger

Anger feels very hot like boiling water being poured over you
Anger makes you want to explode
Anger looks like fire
Anger tastes like boiling chilli
Anger reminds me of my little brother.

Gemma Clarkson (10)
Stonehouse Primary School, Stonehouse

Silence

Silence is white, white as a mouse
Silence sounds like wind, all I can hear
Silence tastes like ice, cold and crisp
Silence looks like a cat, sleeping quiet and soft
Silence feels relaxing, slouching and sleeping
Silence reminds me of my gran's house.

Bethany Hatcher (10)
Stonehouse Primary School, Stonehouse

Anger

Anger is red like a hot sauce
Anger sounds like thunder roaring in the sky
Anger tastes like hot spicy curry
Anger looks like a lion's mane on fire
Anger feels like an uncontrollable horse
Anger reminds me about a football match.

Craig Boyd (10)
Stonehouse Primary School, Stonehouse

Anger

Anger, anger is red like the teacher roaring at me
Anger sounds like thunder crashing in the sky
Anger tastes like red-hot spicy chillies
Anger looks like flickering fire in the night sky
Anger feels very humid.

Lynsey Quinn (10)
Stonehouse Primary School, Stonehouse

Anger

Anger is red like the teacher roaring at me
And it sounds like a lion roaring at its enemy
It tastes like hot, spicy sauce freshly made
It is the hottest in the world
It looks like fire glaring in the night
It feels like burning in your heart
It reminds me of my fight for Scotland at tae kwon do.

Jamie Biggar (10)
Stonehouse Primary School, Stonehouse

Anger

I met anger in my bed
It dragged me and dragged me until it was in me
Its colour is red, as red as it can be
I hate to have anger inside of me
It tastes like a whole pinch of salt in my mouth
Dissolving its way to more anger
It sounds like a thundercloud
I do hate anger, I do, I do
Anger looks like blood burning
I wish this hot bag of spicy chillies
Was out of me instead of in me
It reminds me of the worst thing on Earth . . .
My school, my school, my school.

Ciaran Grant (10)
Stonehouse Primary School, Stonehouse

Silence

Silence is black and white
It is very quiet and it tastes cold
It looks like black and white swirls and is comfortable
It reminds me of my dog sitting in her bed waiting for her dinner.

Michael Evans (10)
Stonehouse Primary School, Stonehouse

Chips

C hips are great
H aving them all the time.
I like salt on my chips
P eople like vinegar on chips
S ome like chops, others don't.

Gary Ferrie (11)
Victoria Primary School, Airdrie

Teacher, Teacher

Teacher, teacher,
You made a fool of me.
You called me a big stuck-up bully.
You rang my dad
And made me sad.
So now I'm gonna get
My payback.
I'll throw my work around the room,
I'll eat my lunch with my mouth opened wide,
Then I'll throw you in the Clyde.

Jordan Hill (11)
Victoria Primary School, Airdrie

Water

Water, water,
I like water.
Who doesn't?
My cousin
And
Steven
Hate water,
I don't mind.

Clark Jarvie (10)
Victoria Primary School, Airdrie

Brother

B ig
R oary
O ften on his bike
T ough
H is name is Mark
E nergetic
R ighteous.

Glen Goldie (10)
Victoria Primary School, Airdrie

The Very Weird Boy

There once was a very weird boy,
He wasn't poor, wasn't rich, but he only had one toy.
Even though he lived in the streets
He had all the joy.
But then one day he found a lottery ticket,
He won £1 million and bought himself a wicket.
He paid for lessons
And now you know it,
He can play very, very good cricket.

James McGuinness (11)
Victoria Primary School, Airdrie

Chocolate Cake

I love chocolate cake
Sitting on my plate.
I love the taste of it
More than a bit.
All I do is take it for lunch
And
Munch! Munch! Munch!

Lee McGuire (11)
Victoria Primary School, Airdrie

Me And My Friends

Me and my friends
Share lots of fun in a day.
We like to run, jump and play
We like to cause mischief in every way.
When we have to go, it's a shame
Because every night it's always the same!

Karly Rae (11)
Victoria Primary School, Airdrie

My Corner

As I walk down the stairs with my play piece in hand
Everyone's running and jumping like mad.
I walk to my corner but someone is there
I have nowhere to go, nowhere to play
What am I to do?
No one cares
I move across to the end of the playground
Where can I sit in peace?
I hear people shouting,
'Geek, freak.'
Are they talking to me?
Where do I go?
I have to hide, quick, quick, run inside.
I go to the toilets to be alone
So that everyone will leave me on my own.

Another day, another challenge
I wonder what corner I will be at today?

Chelsey Lafferty (11)
Victoria Primary School, Airdrie

Lovely Sweets

Sweets
Sweets are tasty
Sweets are good
They put you in a very good mood
But when you get cavities
You will be in a very bad mood.

Raymond Kwok (11)
Victoria Primary School, Airdrie

Twinkle, Twinkle

Twinkle, twinkle,
Fizzy bar,
My dad bought
A banged-up car.
When he put the key in
And tapped the choke
It went bang
With a puff of smoke.
So twinkle, twinkle,
Fizzy bar,
My dad no longer
Has a banged-up car.

Alan Bruce (11)
Victoria Primary School, Airdrie

Dads

D ads are one of the best things in the world
A ll the time they're winding you up, but they really do love you
D aft, my dad is really daft
S imply the best is my dad.

Lucy Haviland (11)
Victoria Primary School, Airdrie

Dads

Dads can be funny.
Dads can be sunny.
But sometimes they can be moody.
But after all I do love my dad.
So that's why I am my daddy's girl.

Kumval Aziz (11)
Victoria Primary School, Airdrie

The Troll Man

There once was a man who turned into a troll,
On Thursday morning when he went out for a stroll.

When he got back to his house, he switched on the telly
But he couldn't see it because of his green, overgrown belly!

So he turned on the radio and listened to the news,
It said a troll had been stomping around Black Avenue.

He thought, *well I live there*
But why was everyone giving me a stare?

Then suddenly it dawned on him, he must be the troll,
It must have happened in the morning when he went out for a stroll.

From then on he lived alone in his shed
And sadly, last week, he was reported dead.

Amy Hollingsworth (11)
Wallace Hall Primary School, Thornhill

Football

There is a game called 'Football',
Where all Italians love to dive and crawl.

In the World Cup 2006,
Zidane and Materazzi were a bunch of twits!

There was no better goal than Joe Cole's,
He chested, then he volleyed, and what a goal by golly!

The winners took all the glory,
I wonder what'll happen in the next World Cup?
But that's another story . . .

Benjamin Goodrich (11)
Wallace Hall Primary School, Thornhill

Monster Truck

All the blood came flying like a water fountain from the driver's seat
The pumpkin sign was orange and gleaming on the bonnet
The diesel smell made me feel sick
My hand touched something rubbery in the very big exhaust
I could hear screaming from the engine
And crackling bones from underneath
Run away now!

Alex Jardine (10)
Whitehirst Park Primary School, Kilwinning

Number Thirteen

In the house of number 13
You will smell dampness and dog
You will hear screaming from the bathroom
And creaking floorboards above you
Burning fires in the bedroom
You will see lights swinging around
And shadows on the cupboards and walls
You'll be lucky to get out!

Laura Macnair (9)
Whitehirst Park Primary School, Kilwinning

666 Hell House

In the house you will hear the spirits of the Underworld moaning
And the Grim Reaper collecting souls
You will hear the howl of a werewolf
You will see blood rushing down the walls
And carcasses hanging from the ceiling
You will touch carcasses that have mould and maggots
You will taste the smell of horror!

Callum Boyle (10)
Whitehirst Park Primary School, Kilwinning

25 Killer Street

As he hit 25 Killer Street's door . . .
He heard footsteps
Worrying slamming doors
Car engines
Then he went in
He saw . . .
Flashing lights
Weapons on the floor
Blackbirds on the roof

And then upstairs
He touched
Spider cobwebs
A hand in the wall
A rocking chair.

Connor Stevenson (10)
Whitehirst Park Primary School, Kilwinning

The Dead House

In the house . . .
You will see a shadow in the window
Something staring at you sternly
The dead house made of wood can see you in every movement
It's like it's alive, no one ever went in and came back.

In the house . . .
You will feel the touch of somebody or something on your shoulder
The touch will be funny but then that's always bad
I never want to go in the house and I never will.

Graham Shield (9)
Whitehirst Park Primary School, Kilwinning

Darkness Castle

In my house I smell a burning body
I taste blood
I touch a bat's wing
I see an old dusty chair
I hear a low moaning sound in the kitchen.

I once saw a spider the size of my hand
I once saw blood on the dishes
I once heard a slamming door though no one was there
There were creaky floorboards in my room.

In my house I felt a shape in the bed
There was a hand on a spider's web.

At Darkness Castle nothing's what it seems.

Sam Hogg (10)
Whitehirst Park Primary School, Kilwinning

The Curse of Candran Castle

In my house, Candran Castle, there is a curse
You will hear the haunted laugh of the Jack-in-the-box
and a scream every four hours
You will see nothing at first, then you will see the creatures
from your worst nightmare
You will taste rotting cheese in the air and rotting carcasses
in your mouth
You can feel the blood stopping to flow
Then you will be destroyed!
You will be destroyed and I and my minions will take over the world.

Stuart Faulkner (10)
Whitehirst Park Primary School, Kilwinning

The Dark Mansion

In the mansion . . .
You will see a bright light flashing in your eyes
A bat flying into your face
A drop of blood in the corner.

In the mansion . . .
You will hear the floorboards creaking
The sound of a door slams
A scream getting louder and louder.

In the mansion . . .
You will smell something cooking
Smoke coming down the chimney
A fire burning well.

The mansion has sixteen rooms
But most of them *are haunted!*

Megan Rainey (9)
Whitehirst Park Primary School, Kilwinning

The Story

In Manhill Manor he heard the sound of freaky slamming doors
A fire crackling and the sound of a creaking staircase
He saw all the lights flickering in all of the rooms
A brick flying through one of the windows with a message saying,
'I'm back!'

Then he felt his face tangled in the mysterious silk of a cobweb
Then he walked towards a room with a closed door
The hard wood flooring collided with his shaking body
As he tripped over someone or something
And then he was winded as if a pole smacked his stomach
He was never seen again
Terrifying because, it's me!

Craig Bruce (10)
Whitehirst Park Primary School, Kilwinning

Mystery Manor

In the house you will hear
Doors slamming behind you as you walk away
Pots crashing in the kitchen, *bang!*
Creaking floors when you're not even standing on them.

In the house you will see
A rocking chair rocking with nobody on it
Lights flashing but who was it?
Keys on the piano moving but no sound.

In the house you will feel
A hand on your shoulder but no one's there
A furry door handle, argh!

It's not a handle, it's a monster
Run for your life!

Emma Hedley (10)
Whitehirst Park Primary School, Kilwinning

Number 81

The door is open
The windows are smashed
No one lives there
Yet smoke pours from the chimney
At number 81.

For old Mr Staff
Of 81
Has never been seen
Or heard of.

The door knocker hits the door
The only thing that is there
Is a small black cat
At number 81.

At number 81
Nothing is what it seems.

Andrew Whyte (10)
Whitehirst Park Primary School, Kilwinning

46 Ghost House

In the ghost house . . .
You will see lots of bats flying around
Some lights flashing in the hall.

In the ghost house . . .
You will hear rats squeaking
Sounds of bats' wings
Screams coming from the hall
The kettle going on and off.

In the ghost house . . .
You will smell burnt food
Smoke coming from the cooker
And a bottle of oil leaking from down the stairs.

There's only something wrong with it . . .
It's haunted!

Jacqueline Reid (10)
Whitehirst Park Primary School, Kilwinning

46 Creep Street

In the house you will hear cracking walls slamming back and forward
A rat squeaking when dying with blood spreading.

In the house you will see human heads, planks of wood
snapping mysteriously
Spiders' blood pouring towards your feet.

In 46 Creep Street
You will touch slimy cobwebs going through your hand
You'll touch a human head and its nose and ears fall off
Run for it!
You'd not want to be in there!

Adam Hodge (9)
Whitehirst Park Primary School, Kilwinning

Number 67

At number 67
There is no doorbell
And one day they heard
Ding-dong! Ding-dong!
They went to the door
And no one was there
And the street was in silence.

The next day
They heard it again
Ding-dong! Ding-dong!
And there were people in the street.

Two weeks later
It went again
And the lady's husband had died
And she went to the door
And all she saw was a gravestone . . .

Kiara Henderson (10)
Whitehirst Park Primary School, Kilwinning

The Scooby-Doo House

Welcome to Scooby-Doo house . . .
You will hear the sounds of bats' wings
Flapping together and creaking floorboards
Ghosts yelping and blood dripping in a corner.

In Scooby-Doo house . . .
You will see a mouldy biscuit with a bite taken out it
And a rocking chair rocking in a black corner.

In Scooby-Doo house . . .
You will feel a monster's hand with spots on it
And something touches you and you scream, 'Argh!'
But you will still return . . .

Gaynor Beaton (10)
Whitehirst Park Primary School, Kilwinning

The Haunted House

The door is dark
Curtains are open
The cat is out
But no one's there
The paint has gone
The grass needs a cut
At number 21.

For old Mrs Dunn
At number 21
They never have the sun
They have rats, bats and cats
At number 21.

The postman never comes
To number 21
I think he's scared
Of old Mrs Dunn
But in the end
She comes out
But it is still strange
At number 21.

Gemma Speirs (10)
Whitehirst Park Primary School, Kilwinning

Number 64

At number 64 you see your shadow
As you twist the door handle
The door slams behind you
Whatever you touch turns you black
As you walk up the stairs
You can hear squeaky floorboards
At the top of the stairs
You can feel dirty cobwebs on your hands.

Chloe McNulty (10)
Whitehirst Park Primary School, Kilwinning

Number 91

The grass needs to be cut
The door is open
The curtains drawn
The lights are off
No one dare open the door.

For old Mr Bun at 91
Never comes out.

The house is brown
There's smashed windows
There is a shadow
I see flashing lights
I hear my name being called
They never see the sun
For old Mr Bun at 91
Is never seen . . .

Lucy Dyson (9)
Whitehirst Park Primary School, Kilwinning

46 Ghost Street

In 46 Ghost Street . . .
I heard bats' wings and they went flying past me very fast
I heard a slamming loud door
I heard someone knocking on the walls.

In 46 Ghost Street . . .
I can see a big whole ghost
I can see a picture with eyes
I can see a flashing light coming from a room.

In 46 Ghost Street . . .
I could touch an old dusty shelf
I could touch a big spider
I could touch a book with spiders' webs.

Rohail Hamid (10)
Whitehirst Park Primary School, Kilwinning

The Creepy House

In the creepy house . . .
You will hear screaming voices every second of the day
And freaky noises such as creaking floorboards in silence
It is scary when you hear the slamming doors shut.

In the creepy house . . .
You will see flashing lights every day through the window
You will see bright red blood dripping down the cream walls
You will see creepy shadows moving very slowly.

In the creepy house . . .
You can touch a slimy wall with snails on it
It was awfully dirty when you touched a grey dusty cobweb
And a head in a dusty grey cobweb.

You would be glad to get out of it!

Fiona McAllister (10)
Whitehirst Park Primary School, Kilwinning

48 The Number That Everyone Must Hate

Every mum, every dad
Hates the man of 48
Anything that goes on his grass
Will be taken in and ripped apart
He is never seen except
When he is covered in sheets of dark
The old man of 48
Disappears in the dark
It will scare your pants off!

Blair Wilson (10)
Whitehirst Park Primary School, Kilwinning

101 Haunt Street

In 101 Haunt Street
I saw a crackling fire burning away with no one in sight
I saw a vicious bloodthirsty rat nibbling at a bit of wood
I saw a strange picture, its eyes were red and trying to look at me.

I heard a small timid voice saying my name over and over again
I heard a whistling sound getting louder and louder
All night I heard screams getting more horrible by the hour.

I was able to feel thick, grey, smelly air in my hands
I felt like I could taste my old friend's scent of perfume who died
three days ago

Nothing is what it seems in 101 Haunt Street!

Jamie Kane (10)
Whitehirst Park Primary School, Kilwinning

Monster House

Inside the monster house
There was something creepy
Inside the monster house
There was a monster's hands
In the monster house
You will see a hand in a cobweb
A flashing light and a shape on the bed
In the monster house
You will touch and feel monster's hands
And something you touch comes alive!

Ross Pilling (10)
Whitehirst Park Primary School, Kilwinning

Bags! Bags! Bags!

Big bags
Small bags
Tesco, Asda, Safeway bags
Plastic, leather, cloth bags
My mum collects a few.

Black bags
Brown bags
Sparkly, beady, shiny bags
Hard, soft, squidgy bags
I buy them too.

Designer bags
Fake bags
Work, party, sporty bags
Last of all, best of all
Are Jane Norman bags.

Amanda Johnston (11)
Woodlands Primary School, Irvine

Flowers! Flowers! Flowers!

Summer flowers
Spring flowers
Lily, roses, iris flowers
Pansies, daffodil, daisy flowers
To name but a few.

Autumn flowers
Winter flowers
Dahlia, begonia, aster flowers
Crocus, lupins, busy Lizzie flowers
All lovely colours too.

Large flowers
Small flowers
Chrysanthemum, nasturtium, gladioli flowers
Last of all, best of all
Snowdrops, poppies, marigold flowers.

Lauren McGill (11)
Woodlands Primary School, Irvine

Horses! Horses! Horses!

Small horses
Tall horses
Giant, saddled-up horses
Tiny, crazy, mucky horses
Boring, old, biting, grumpy few.

Cob horses
Clydesdale horses
Even little Shetland horses
And mighty shire horses
In-between horses too.

Lazy horses
Stubborn horses
Easy, speedy, spooked horses
Last of all, best of all
Cuddly, naughty, cheeky horses.

Louise Miller (11)
Woodlands Primary School, Irvine

Cars! Cars! Cars!

Big cars
Small cars
Blue, silver, red cars
Long, thin, limo cars
We only have a few.

Sports cars
Race cars
Big, bulky, family cars
Really fast F1 cars
We love cars too.

Old cars
Vintage cars
Lots of different coloured cars
Last of all, best of all
Really fast Porsche cars.

Andrew Gow (11)
Woodlands Primary School, Irvine

Cats! Cats! Cats!

Big cats
Small cats
Short, stout, tubby cats
Tall, proud, sleek cats
There always are a few.

White cats
Black cats
Grey, brown, ginger cats
Cream and tabby cats
Maybe pink cats too.

Fluffy cats
Fuzzy cats
Little, cheeky, playful cats
Last of all, best of all
Cute, little, furball cats.

Katie Bremner (10)
Woodlands Primary School, Irvine

Sweets! Sweets! Sweets!

Blue sweets
Yellow sweets
All different coloured sweets
Chewy, soft, hard sweets
There's many, not a few.

Sour sweets
Sweet sweets
All different tasty sweets
Bad-for-teeth sweets
Everybody likes them too.

Chocolate sweets
Fruity sweets
All different kinds of sweets
Last of all, best of all
I love all sweets.

Anthony James Chalmers (11)
Woodlands Primary School, Irvine

My Best Friend

Louise is vibrant, glittery pink
She is a sunny carefree summer
At a sandy beach with clear blue waves
She is a light, sunny, warm day
And a bright colourful dress
An extreme makeover
Louise is a bowl of cream, cold ice cream.

Kimberley Dean (11)
Woodlands Primary School, Irvine

My Dad

My dad is mellow yellow
He is a calm summer's night in a police station
He is a bolt of lightning in a business suit and a tidy house
He is the news and a plate of wobbly jelly.

Rebecca Greenwood (11)
Woodlands Primary School, Irvine

My Brother

My brother is green
He's a temperature-dropping winter morning in an open field
A flash of lightning in a dark sky
He is a football top, a bed not made
He is the 'Weakest Link', a cold plate of peas.

Kyle McDade (11)
Woodlands Primary School, Irvine